This journal belongs to:

_____

"Watch and you'll see,
someday I'll be part of your
world." — Ariel

CRISTIE PUBLISHING

DATE:
_____

DATE:
_____

DATE:
_____

DATE:
_____

DATE:
_____

DATE:
_____

DATE:
_____

DATE:
_____

DATE:
_____

DATE:
_____

DATE:
_____

DATE:
_____

DATE:
_____

DATE:
_____

DATE:
_____

DATE:
_____

DATE:
_____

DATE:
_____

DATE:
_____

DATE:
_____

DATE:
_____

DATE:
_____

DATE:
_____

DATE:
_____

DATE:
_____

DATE:
_____

DATE:
_____

DATE:
_____

DATE:
_____

DATE:
_____

DATE:
_____

DATE:
_____

DATE:
_____

DATE:
_____

DATE:
_____

DATE:
_____

DATE:
_____

DATE:
_____

DATE:
_____

DATE:
_____

DATE:
_____

DATE:
_____

DATE:

_____

DATE:

DATE:
_____

DATE:
_____

DATE:
_____

DATE:
_____

Thank you princess!
I hope you have enjoyed my mermaid write and draw day book.
Please leave a review.

www.ingramcontent.com/pod-product-compliance
Lightning Source LLC
Chambersburg PA
CBHW060103070526
44654CB00051B/1615